HERE COMES THE AEROPLANE!

A guide to building insight with your picky eater.

Moffat Makomo

This is dedicated to my Patience, Luanne and Seth.

CONTENTS

PREFACE

Meal planning and preparation can be an enjoyable and relaxing activity as you experience the calming effects of the sensory experience. The smells, textures, colours, sounds and tastes of the ingredients can bring the much-needed effects to calm us. This experience can be different if you have a picky eaters. Meal planning becomes a tough and impossible task for so many parents. Choosing the right ingredients with the just right right smell, texture, taste, color and even the right brand can be frustrating. The smallest change or difference in how the food is made or how it looks can impact if your child will consume it.

In this book we will explore some ways you can work with your child to improve their insight and yours into why they are picky as well as the parent gaining. This book is meant to be read by the parent and the child together with conversation starters and discussion questions.

ARE YOU HUNGRY?

Tanaka does not seem to notice when he is hungry or thirsty most of the time. Sometimes children do not seem to know when they are hungry. They will have to be told to eat.

Your stomach tells your brain you are hungry when it is empty, when it growls, when we have headaches and we might feel lightheaded or grouchy.

Lets Find Out!

1. How do you know you are hungry?
2. What time do you eat breakfast, lunch and dinner?

CRUNCHY FOOD PLEASE!

Some children prefer specific textures of food and they do not like other textures. They might like eating crunchy foods such as apples, candies, crisps and crunchy chicken nuggets. Parents should identify their child's preferred food textures to increase their chances of eating.

Let's Find Out!

1. Do you like soft, smushy or goey foods?
2. List three foods that you like.

WHAT IS THAT SMELL?

Tanaka does not like certain smells and taste of food. He will move away if he does not like the smell. Smells and tastes of food are important to us. This is what helps us enjoy the food we eat. Try to serve the prefered food tastes for each meal.

Let's Find Out!

1. Why is Tanaka holding his nose?
2. What food smells do you prefer?
3. What food taste do you prefer?

WHAT DO YOU WANT TO EAT?

Tanaka finds it difficult to choose what he wants to eat. He prefers for his mother to tell him what he is going to eat. Sometimes children get overwhelmed when asked to choose what they want to eat. Provide several choices of food the child to choose from.

Let's Find Out!

1. What is happening in the picture?
2. Do you find it difficult to choose what you want to eat?

OH NO!

Tanaka does not like his food mixing in his plate. Each food group must be separate. He uses a plate with sections. If separating foods into sections helps the child eat their food, then go for it.

Let's Find Out!

1. Are you bothered if your food mixes in your plate?
2. Which food do you not like mixing?

MY FAVOURITE

Tanaka's favourite food is pizza from his favourite shop. He loves cheese pizza. Our favourite foods can be calming and soothing when we eat them. Parents can identify their child's comfort foods and add them to the menu planner.

Let's Find Out!

1. What is your favourite food?
2. What is your favourite store to get food?

COMFORT FOOD

We all have comfort food that we eat over and over again to feel relaxed. Comfort foods have a placed value and meaning to the child. Knowing why your child prefers this food can unlock clues that we can use. Use this to expand the range of foods the child can eat, while pairing comfort food with new menus or dishes.

Let's Find Out!

1. Do you know what your comfort food is?
2. How do you feel when you eat it?

CARE SEEKING BEHAVIOUR

Tanaka almost always wants his mother to sit next to him when he is eating. Even when his mother is busy, setting boundaries (your gold standard), have a clear and concise expectation, plan ignore and showing them the appropriate way to seek care.

Let's Find Out!

1. What is happening in this picture?
2. Can you eat your food without someone sitting with you?

FUN WITH MY SISTER

Tanaka likes to do what his big sister does. He tries to eat whatever his sister is eating. Having another adventurous child can help your child try new foods.

Let's Find Out!

1. Do you have a friend or sibling to look up to?
2. Have you tried new foods because of them?
3. Do you think it would help if that friend or sibling encouraged you?

FOOD GAMES

Tanaka and his mother always have fun playing games with food. This can be designing shapes with fruits or molding animals with flour dough. Fun games are good as they help to create positive lasting memories. We learn better when we are enjoying what we are doing.

Let's Find Out!

1. What is happening in the picture?
2. What fun food activities do you like playing?

ACKNOWLEDGEMENT

I would like to thank my Seth, Luanne and Patiencewho are the inspiration for writing this book. You guys are the best.

ABOUT THE AUTHOR

Moffat Makomo

Moffat Makomo is a Paediatric Occupational therapist for the last 16 years. He has worked in Zimbabwe, Egypt, Bermuda and now Manchester (UK). Moffat is also a father who has one daughter and one son: Luanne and Seth. He has been married to his wife, Patience, for 10 years. He is a brother too with three brothers and three sisters. In his free time, chess, reading, playing games, listening to music, and going for walks are his pastimes. In the year ahead, Moffat looks forward to writing, sharing information, and developing his own interest and skill at writing.

Printed in Great Britain
by Amazon

64565973R00017